Mel Bay's
Guitar *deluxe* Position studies *by Roger Filiberto*

Before any student of the guitar can advance, he must eventually learn to perform well in higher fingerboard positions. Position studies are an essential ingredient in building technique and in developing ability in reading music. This text is a thorough study into position playing and is a supplement to Grade II of the Mel Bay *Modern Guitar Method* and to the Mel Bay *Classic Guitar Method,* Vol. II.

Mel Bay

1 2 3 4 5 6 7 8 9 0

Visit us on the Web at www.melbay.com — E-mail us at email@melbay.com

ROGER FILIBERTO

AUTHOR'S NOTE

The study of positions is very important and necessary to the serious student. You will move along slowly and methodically in the beginning. This is to be expected. Through Grades One and Two the student has learned more or less, a fixed fingering and has by this time established good reading habits and reflexes.

Now, it is almost as if you are beginning again. However, it is in a new and very important phase which will ultimately lead to a broader knowledge of the instrument and the development of a skill bordering on the professional level.

Putting it squarely to the student and in the most simple language: "Learning the positions is a MUST if you are ever to become expert on the Guitar".

Roger Filiberto

THE SECOND POSITION

The student should be thoroughly familiar with all of the notes in this position as only the second through fifth frets are involved. The most important thing to remember is that there are NO OPEN STRINGS in position studies. A scale chart of all of the notes in 2nd position is pictured here: observe fingering carefully.

Notes in the Second Position

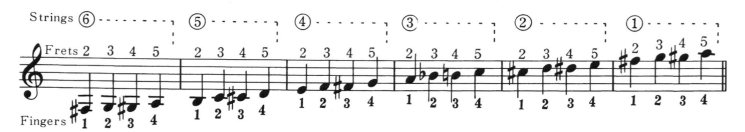

When practicing the position studies that follow it is important that you use the fingering as indicated above.

The best keys for second position are G major and D major. Next is the key of A major and last is the key of C major. The scales of G and D major stay in 2nd position on all strings. The scale of A major departs from 2nd position briefly because of the G♯ at the 1st fret of the 3rd string. The scale in the key of C major is the most awkward because of the F note on the 6th fret of the B or 2nd string.

Complete Scale of D Major in Second Position

Second Position Etude No. 1

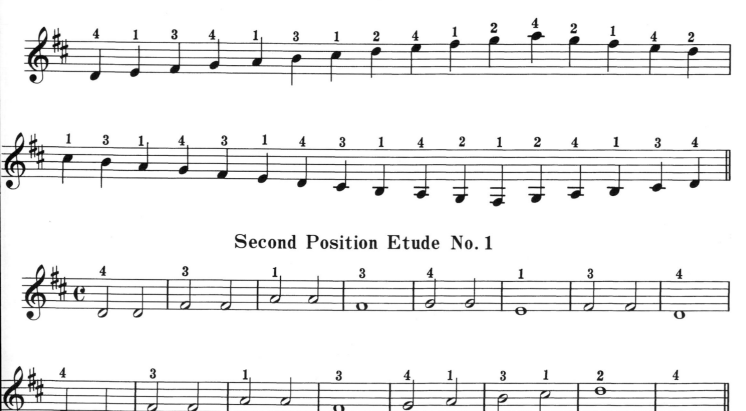

4

My Bonnie
Second Position Etude No. 2

Second Position Etude No. 3

Second Position Etude No. 4

Second Position Etude No. 5

America, the Beautiful
Second Position Etude No. 6

Samuel A. Ward

Complete Scale of C Major in Second Position

Second Position Etude No. 7

Complete Scale of A Major in Second Position

Folk Song
Second Position Study in A Major

Old Folks at Home
Second Position Etude in C Major

Arpeggio Study in Second Position

8

Parts one and two are played exactly alike. In part two we merely substitute two eighth notes for the quarter notes in part one in order to facilitate the counting.

Syncopation - in D (Second Position)

For those of you who have neglected the study and practice of SYNCOPATION there will be a few pages occasionally inserted in this book in order to help you.

These studies will be given to you in the position which you are studying and will prove valuable to you.

Review (Second Position. Keys of G, C, A)

Tempo di Marcia

Second Position Scale Study in G Major

Play this study five times.

More Second Position Study in G Major

Tramp! Tramp! Tramp! (Second Position)

Fingering and string marking omitted.

Geo. F. Root

Marcia

9

Hexicana

"with a Latin beat"

A Study in Second Position

Easy swing -with relaxed feeling.

★ Observe the "Slur" at this particular point.

THE THIRD POSITION

Scale Chart of All Notes in Third Position

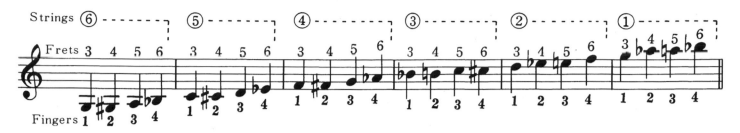

The best keys for the 3rd position are A♭ major and E♭ major. Next is the key of B♭ major and last is the key of D♭. The scales of A♭ and E♭ major stay in 3rd position on all strings. The scale of B♭ major departs from 3rd position briefly because of the A at the 2nd fret of the 3rd string.   The scale in the key of D♭ major is the most awkward because of the G♭ note on the 7th fret of the B or 2nd string.

Complete Scale of B♭ Major in Third Position

On Top of Old Smoky

B♭ Waltz-Third Position

By this time it is more than likely that the student may want some questions answered regarding positions. Listed below are the questions most likely to be brought up.

No. 1 Can a tune be played in more than one position?
A tune **can** be played in more than one position.
Ex: See "Waltz in B♭" on the next page.

No. 2 Do you ever depart from the usual notes studied in the positions thus far?
Yes! See "March in B♭" on the next page. More examples will be shown later in this book.

No. 3 How do you determine what position to play in?
It will be necessary to learn all of the positions through the ninth before this question can be satisfactorily answered. However, it is possible to make a choice when you have completed the 5th position studies.

Elaborating further on question #2 you will note that in the "March in B♭" you have an "A" in the third complete measure (see *). Actually this "A" is out of position but can be played by remaining in 3rd position and extending the first finger back to the 2nd fret, still keeping the left hand thumb parallel with the 3rd fret. This movement is **not** difficult and can be easily mastered after a few attempts. Your teacher can direct you on a proper course at this time.

March in B♭ -Introducing "A" on Third String

★ Keep the left hand thumb parallel with the 3rd fret and simply "slide" the first finger back to the 2nd fret to play the "a" note. A more detailed explanation will be found on page 33 upon introducing the extended 5th position scale.

Down in the Valley
Waltz in B♭ -Using Third and Second Positions

★ The above study is played entirely in the 3rd position with the exception of the 7th measure which is in 2nd position.

Syncopation in B♭
A Scale Study in Third Position

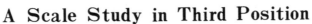

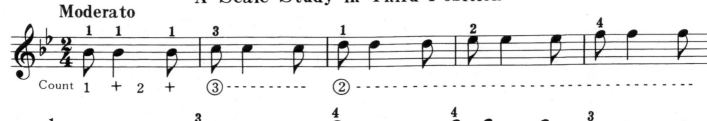

Study in Third Position

★ In these two measures the quarter note with a dot is substituted for the eighth tied to a quarter note in the other measures.

The Complete E♭ Major Scale in Third Position

Third Position Study in E♭ Major

Ballad style

More in B♭-Third Position

Maestoso

Our next study will use all six strings. Review the complete B♭ major scale in 3rd position.

Allegro

★ Occasionally you will be confronted with similar situations. For smoother fingering we recommend using the 4th finger on the "A" note, then sliding to the B♭ with same finger.

More in E♭-Third Position

Waltz tempo

J. S. Bach

The following short study is a perfect example of changing positions. In the 4th measure you are actually in 5th position. In measure #5 you shift back to the 3rd position and in the last measure you end in 2nd position.

Rock of Ages
A Combination of Second and Third Position

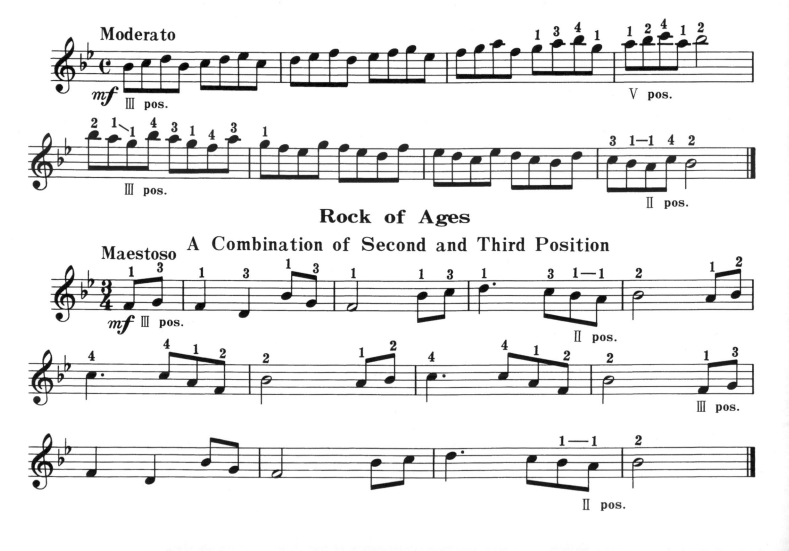

Third Position Etude

The above scale and chord arpeggio study should also help the development of sight reading. The scales and arpeggios are easily identified. A good knowledge of chord spelling will speed up your sight reading by anticipating chordal tones.

Third Position Etude

The real value of scale studies is in the development of velocity. We suggest the use of the method "Guitar Technic" for further improvement in velocity and developing the strength of the fingers.

The Complete A♭ Major Scale in Third Position

Country Gardens
A Third Position Study in A♭

The Merry Widow Waltz
Third Position Study

A♭ Scale in Third Position

Triplet Etude in A♭ -Third Position

THE FOURTH POSITION

Below is a scale chart of all the notes in this position

The most frequently used keys in the 4th position are A major and E major. Next is the key of B major and last is the key of D. The scales of A and E major stay in 4th position on all strings. The scale of B major departs from the 4th position briefly because of the A♯ at the third fret of the third string. The scale in the key of D major is the most awkward because of the G note on the 8th fret of the B or 2nd string.

British Grenadiers

A study in 4th position using the first three strings only.

★ Observe the L. H. fingering in the 9th and 11th measures.

Fourth Position Etude

Another study using the first three strings only.

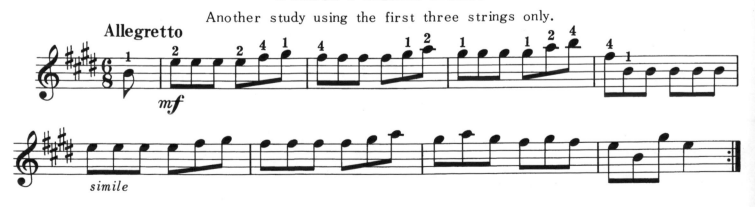

Red River Valley

A study in 4th position using the first three strings only.

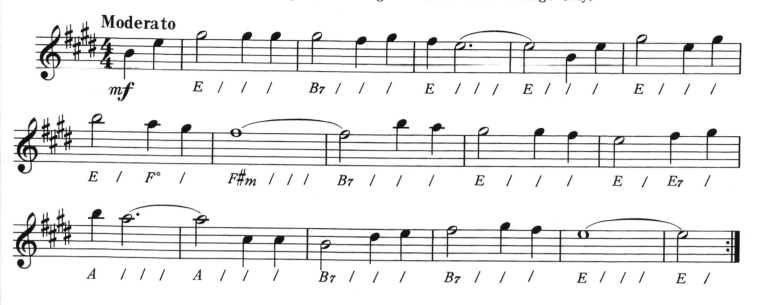

Flow Gently, Sweet Afton

More in 4th position using the first three strings only.

The Complete Scale of E Major in Fourth Position

E Major Etude in Fourth Position

Fourth Position Scale Study

The Complete Scale of A Major in Fourth Position

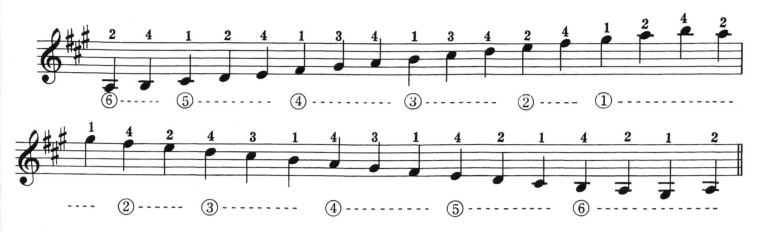

Fourth Position Study in A Major

Observe the 4/8 time signature.

★ Take note of unusual fingering in 3rd, 6th, 11th & 14th measures.

Rondo in E Major-Fourth Position Study

Allegretto

Mazas

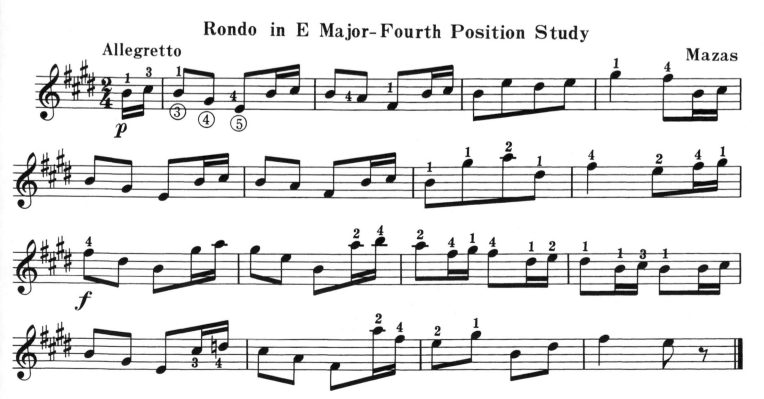

Fisher's Hornpipe
Fourth Position Study

★ Normally this "A" note would beplayed with the 2nd finger.   However, in this particular   situation it is much smoother to play this note with the 3rd finger.

Fourth Position Scale Study in the Key of A Major

Triplet Study A Major-Fourth Position

Fourth Position Etude
Key of A Major

Fourth Position-Key of A Major
Excerpt from "Pleyel Duets"

★ Play the 5th & 6th, 15th & 16th, 24th & 25th measures in 2nd position. These measures can be played in 4th position but it is much more practical and smoother in 2nd position.

More in Fourth Position-Key of A Major

Fourth Position Study
Greensleeves

Traditional English
Folk Song

Observe the shift to Third Position in the 14th, 30th, 31st & 32nd measures.

Fourth Position Study in A Major

Guitar Duet

Country Life

This study appears in the Mel Bay Grade Three in 1st position.

Mazas
Arr. by Mel Bay

THE FIFTH POSITION

All positions from the Second position to the Fifth position are important and useful. However, particular emphasis is placed on the Fifth position because it is in this position that the student becomes fully acquainted with "Identical" notes. *(See example below.) At this stage of learning, the student who has reached Grade Three already knows all of the notes through the fifth fret. This is why the Fifth position now assumes such importance.

The next few pages will be devoted to the study of the C major scale, one octave only, showing the notes from C in the third space of the staff to the C above. You will be given enough easy work to establish a good foundation in this position. Progress will be slow in the beginning. This is to be expected. Through Grades One and Two, the student has learned a fixed fingering and by this time has established good reading habits and reflexes. Now, it is almost like starting all over again, but in a new and more important phase which will ultimately lead to a broader knowledge of the instrument and the development of a skill bordering on the professional level.

The most frequently used keys in this position are, Bb major, F major and C major. The key of Eb major is also a possibility, but it is awkward to execute and therefore seldom if ever used in this position.

*Identical Note Chart

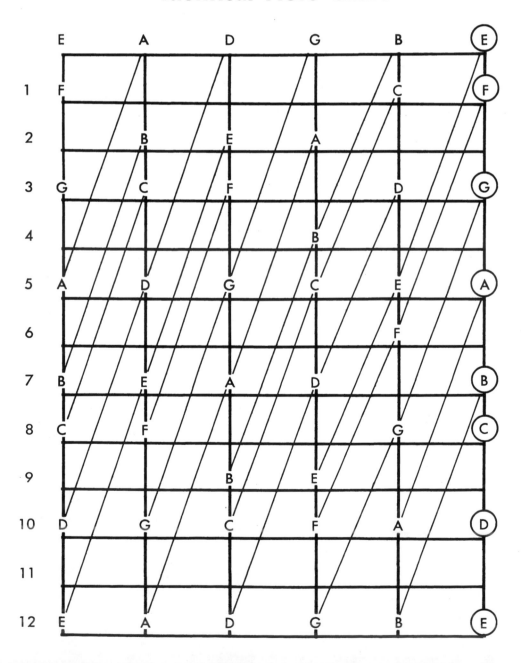

THE FIFTH POSITION

The C Major Scale
One Octave only

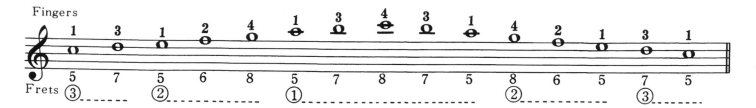

Fifth Position Study No. 1

Slowly

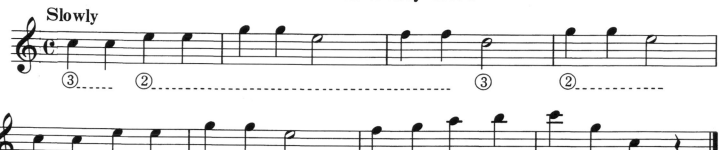

Fifth Position Study No. 2

Moderato

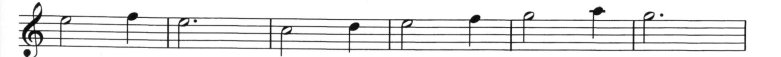

Fifth Position Study No. 3

Slow

Fifth Position Study No. 4

Fifth Position Study No. 5

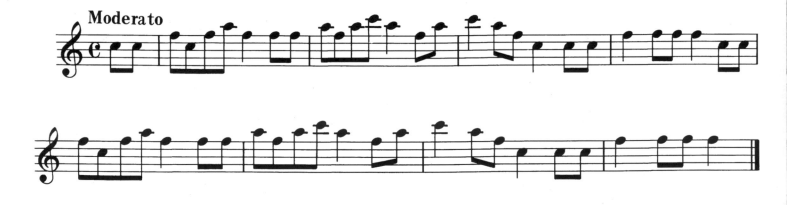

Fifth Position Study No. 6

Fifth Position Study No. 7

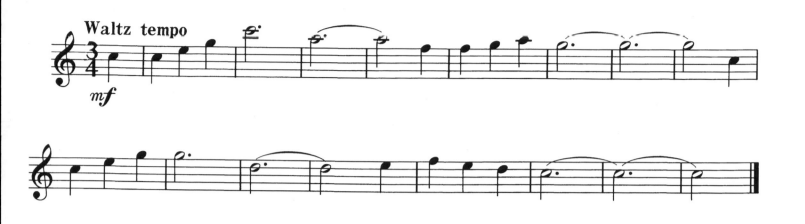

Fifth Position Study No. 8

Fifth Position Study No. 9

Fifth Position Study No. 10

Fifth Position Study No. 11

This is a 5th position study in "syncopation." If you have trouble reading "syncopation", look for detailed explanation on how to read syncopation on page no. 8

Fifth Position Study No. 12

The Extended Fifth Position

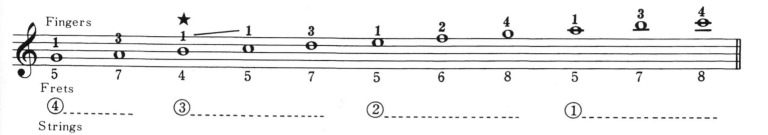

★ Introducing the "B" note on the 4th fret of the G or 3rd string.

Good, steady practice of the scale in 5th position will improve your technic, but will not do much to aid your reading. Reading will only improve by playing tunes, beginning with simple songs at first, gradually moving to more difficult ones as your reflexes improve. That is the only solution. Progress will be slow at first, but improvement will come in time. Be patient. Success comes only to those who are tenacious and persistent.

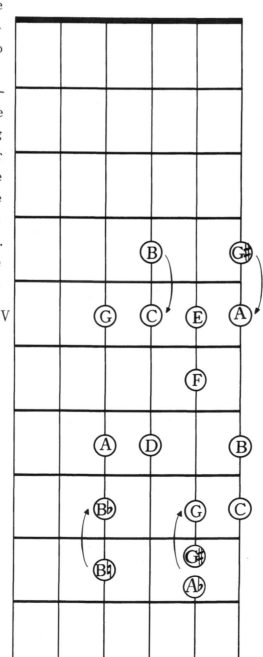

The B and G♯ at the fourth fret are not part of 5th position. When moving from B to C both of these notes should be played with the 1st finger. The same rule will apply to the movement of G♯ to A.

Both B and G♯ can be played at the 9th fret. When the B moves downward to B♭ and the G♯ appears as an A♭ moving downward to G these notes should be played at the 9th fret moving downward chromatically to the 8th fret, using the 4th finger to execute this movement.

Home on the Range

Fifth position study covering the 1st four strings.

★ Note the introduction of F♯ ··· here it is just a part of a chromatic passage from E to G.

The use of B to C on the third string occurs numerous times in this lesson. A word of caution is wise and timely now. In all position work, the thumb parallels the 1st finger, generally speaking. However, when moving back to the 4th fret for the "B" note you should retain the thumb at the 5th fret. The same rule should apply if extending the 4th finger to the 9th fret. Always keep the thumb parallel with the 5th fret.

An aid to reading "syncopation."

Fifth Position Study

Guitar 1 and Guitar 2 are played exactly the same way. See example and explanation of syncopation appearing earlier in this book.

★ Quarter note in Guitar 1 is replaced by two tied eighth notes in Guitar 2.

★★ Sixth and Fourteenth measures are played in the Fourth position.

Continuing the Extended Fifth Position

Adding the B♭ on 1st string and introducing the "G♯" on the 4th fret,
1st string, and playing it with the 1st finger.

Fifth Position Chromatic Etude in C Major

★ Observe the use of the D♯ to E on the 2nd string. This follows the same pattern and use of
the 1st finger in all chromatic situations of this kind. Although the notes are different, there is
nothing new in this pattern. Student should also take notice of the "blues" feeling and "riff style"
of this particular figure.

Nobody Knows The Trouble I've Seen
More Syncopation in Fifth Position

Spiritual

★ Tied eighth notes are substituted in the 17th, 19th and 21st measures for the quarter notes in the 1st, 3rd and 5th measures.

The Fifth Position Complete

All of the notes from the 5th fret through the Eighth fret on all the strings.

Study No. 1

Slow waltz

★ See page 33.

Study No. 2

Solid four

* See explanation on page 33.

Velocity studies in Fifth Position. Practice slowly at first, increasing speed gradually as you become more familiar with this position.

> Accent sign

Fifth Position Etude No. 1

Fifth Position Etude No. 2

★ This high "D" note is out of 5th Position. Pay particular attention to the fingering. Use the 4th finger ascending, and the 2nd finger descending.

Fifth Position Study

Syncopation studies for Guitar showing equivalent time values.

Ex. 1

Count 1 + 2 + 3 + 4   *simile*

Count 1 + 2 + 3 + 4   *simile*

Ex. 2

1 + 2 + 3 + 4

1 + 2 + 3 + 4

Ex. 3

1 + 2 + 3 + 4 +

1 + 2 + 3 + 4 +

Ex. 4

1 + 2 + 3 + 4 +

1 + 2 + 3 + 4 +

In Ex. 1 the tied eighth notes in the lower staff are played exactly the same as the quarter note in the upper staff. Examples 2, 3 & 4, are merely variations of the same pattern. Syncopation is easy to master but requires an honest effort on the student's part.

The A Minor Scale (Harmonic) in Second and Third Positions

Scale No. 1

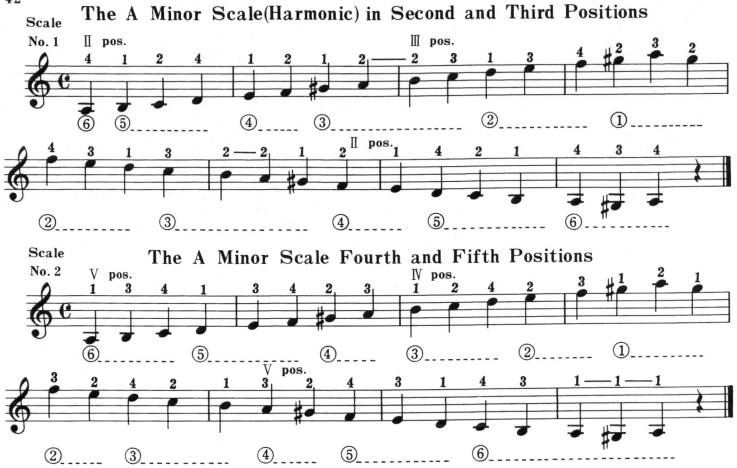

The A Minor Scale Fourth and Fifth Positions

Scale No. 2

These two A minor Scales are identical. They are, however, answer to a previous query. Compositions, scales, studies, etc., position.

played differently and provide the can be played in more than one

Practice the following study using the fingering as shown in scale No. 1 and then as a separate study using the fingering in scale No. 2.

A Minor Study No. 1

Moderato

A Minor Study No. 2

Allegretto   (Use scale No. 2)

Continuing the Fifth Position Study

Fifth Position Study

Russian Melody

Fifth Position Etude on 6th, 5th, 4th Strings

Goofin' off
For three Guitars

An Original
by
Roger Filiberto

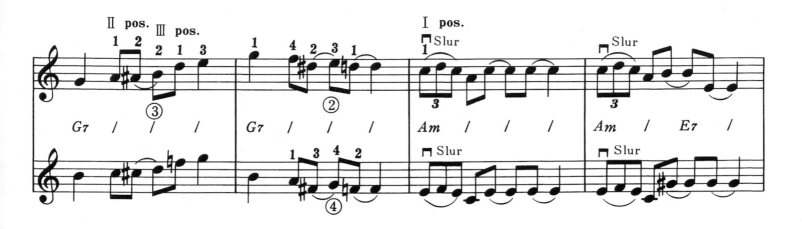

Minuetto
Fifth Position Study in B♭ Major

I. Pleyel Opus 48
Arr. by Mel Bay

Complete B♭ Major Scale in Fifth Position
Using All Strings

Fifth Position Etude in B♭

Fifth Position Etude in B♭

My Maryland

Jazz Version, Three Guitars

Turkey In The Straw

Lively

American Folk Song

The student will select the position in which to play "Turkey in the Straw." How will I know which position to play this tune? How do I find out? These questions were left unanswered earlier in this book. The key in which a selection is written is most important. This composition is written in the key of C. The positions (already introduced) most suitable for this key are the 2nd and 5th.

How do I determine which of these two positions is the proper one or the best one. The highest note is usually the most important clue after establishing the key. This system of selecting the position is the most practical and will prove correct in most instances. No fingering is suggested and the reason is obvious. It's up to you.

Highest note in 2nd position

Highest note in 5th position

More Fifth Position Studies
Three tunes in the Key of F Major

No fingering is suggested. The student should know this position well enough at this stage to make the markings un-necessary.

V pos.
Drink to Me Only With Thine Eyes

Andante

English Air

V pos.
Silent Night, Holy Night

Moderato

Franz Gruber

V pos. ### Believe Me, If All Those Endearing Young Charms

Moderato

Moore

"D Minor" Frolic-Syncopation Study in the Fifth Position

Dark Eyes
Fifth Position Study-Two Guitars
(Ochi Tchornia)

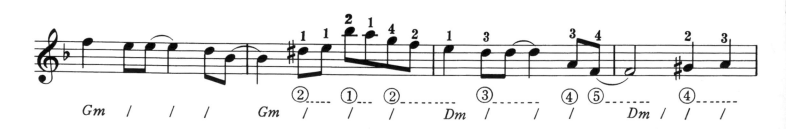

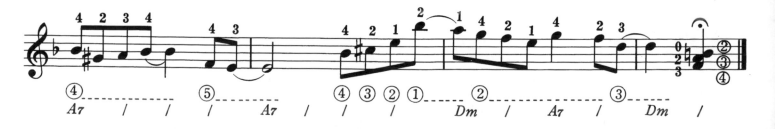

How About That
Syncopation Study for Guitar in Fifth Position

An original by
Roger Filiberto

Notice frequent use of tied notes, particularly in sections A and C (release) giving this tune a feeling of "free" and "easy" swing.

American Patrol
Fifth Position Study in Syncopation (For Three Guitars)

THE SEVENTH POSITION
The D Major Scale-One Octave Only

Seventh Position Study No. 1

Seventh Position Study No. 2-Key of G Major

Seventh Position Study No. 3

Seventh Position Study No. 4

Seventh Position Study No. 5

Seventh Position Study No. 6

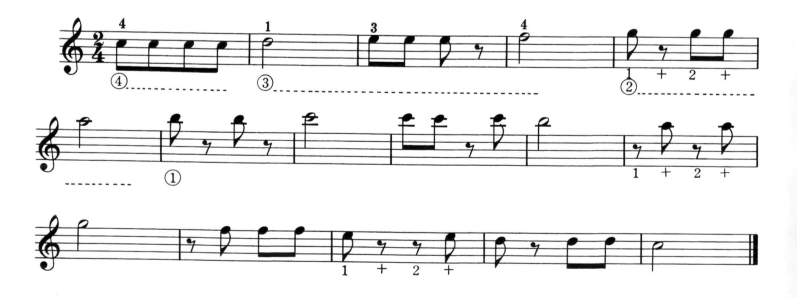

Expanding the Seventh Position
Now including the Fourth String

Minuetto

Moderato

R. De Visée

Beautiful Dreamer

D. S. al Fine

★ Observe the C♯ in the 4th and 15th measure··· play this note with the 1st finger. Take care to keep the L. H. Thumb parallel with the 7th fret. See previous explanation referring to this movement in the 5th position.

Three Alla Breve Studies
(Cut time)

No. 1

No. 2

No. 3

There is A Tavern in The Town
Seventh Position Study

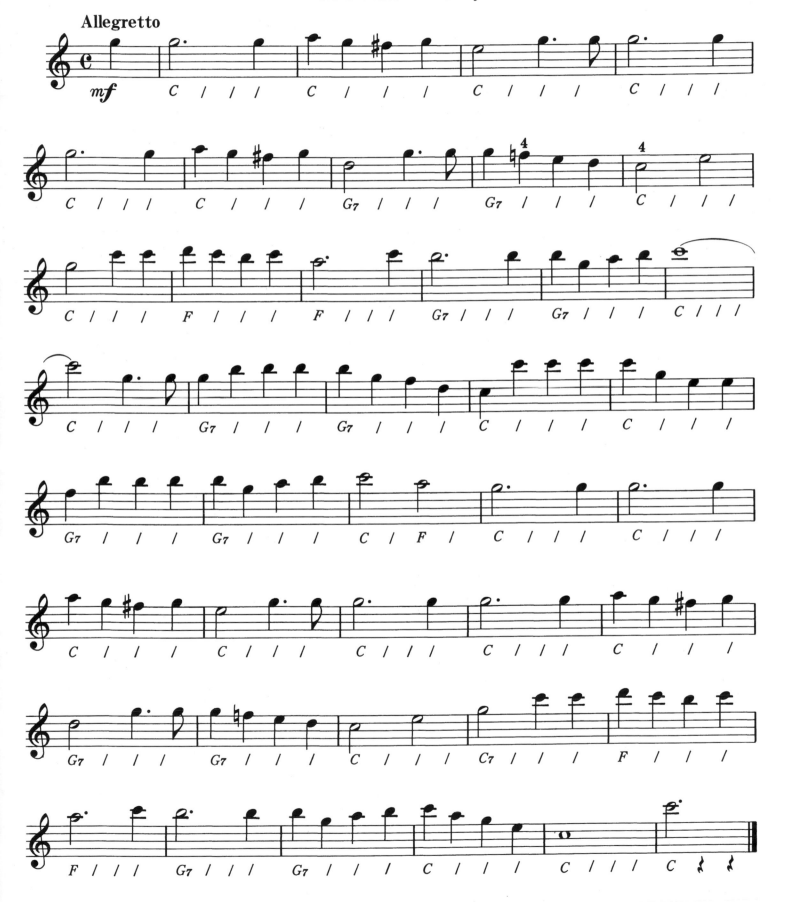

Rock of Ages
Seventh Position Study

Aloha Oe

The Seventh Position Complete

All of the notes from the seventh fret through the tenth fret on all of the strings.

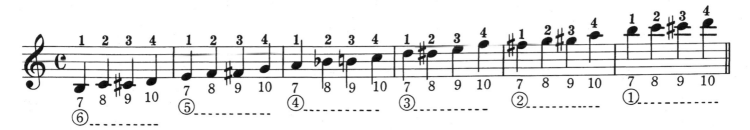

G Major Etude - Seventh Position

D Major Etude - Seventh Position

Home On The Range
Seventh Position Study

This tune appeared previously as a study in the Extended Fifth Position.   In that position it was necessary to play the "B" note, third line of the staff, with the 1st finger, actually out of position.

However, in this, the 7th position, all notes fall in their proper places, without any extension "out of position" as in the 5th.

As for this tune, it is possible to play it in either 5th or 7th position. Either way is correct, leaving the choice of position to the students. This is in answer to a previous question "Can a tune be played in more than one position." Obviously, it CAN.

Seventh Position Study
Menuett II

★ Observe the G♯ in the 5th, 11th and 23rd measures, and the C♯ in the 7th measure. Play these notes with the L. H. 1st finger while retaining the L. H. thumb parallel with the 7th fret. Remember the rule explaining this particular situation in 5th position.

Syncopation Study Seventh Position - Key of C Major

Ex. 1 and 2 are played the same way, although written differently.

Gavotte
From the Fifth French Suite
(Seventh Position)

Moderato

J. S. Bach

At this point it would be well to review quickly what you have learned. Not in actual practice but in analyzing the different positions and their relationship to the composition.

This fine Bach Gavotte can be played in 1st, 2nd, 5th and 7th positions.   In the first and second positions there will be many "trouble" spots. Reaching up to "B" and "C" on the first string will involve shifting of positions and will not look very professional. The 5th position will be better than the 1st and 2nd Positions and can be a possible choice. Fingering will come out fairly well, however uncomfortable at times.

The 7th position, as you will see, will be best for this Bach work. With the exception of the   slide back to C♯ with the 1st finger in the 6th complete measure and the temporary detour to 6th position in the 4th complete measure of the 2nd part,   the 7th position is the smoothest and most comfortable.

Try it in all above mentioned positions and you be the judge. It is this sort of thing that will do the most to develop your knowledge and help you in future choices of positions.

E Minor Scale-Seventh Position

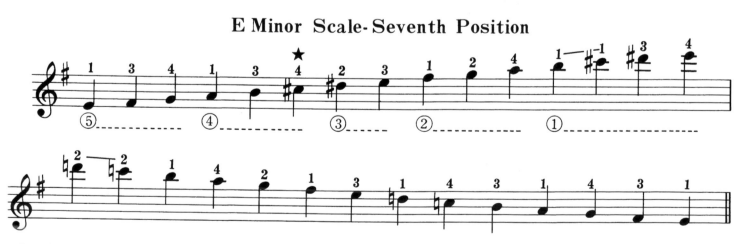

★ This extension of the 4th finger is contrary to what we have previously suggested, but in this particular case it is the smoothest and most comfortable way. Also, the frets are narrower at the 7th position than in 1st to 3rd positions, and one must not be so confined to rules as to lose all sense of being practical.

Irish Jig
Seventh Position Study

★ Notice the shift to 8th position by using the 1st finger on the C note at the 8th fret in order to reach the High E on the 12th fret firmly and accurately. This particular passage may be played by staying in 7th position, using the 2nd finger on the C at the 8th fret, then after reaching for high E with 4th finger, play the D on the 10th fret with 2nd finger, gliding back to C on 8th fret with the same (2nd) finger, bringing you back solidly into the seventh position. Either fingering is correct. Use whichever is most comfortable and accurate for you.

Observe effective use of the slur  . Play the second note of all slurs with left hand pizzicato ("pulling" the string).

Allegro - Seventh Position

Progressive Jazz for Three Guitars
Little Brown Jug

The Ash Grove
Seventh Position Study

Rondo

Allegretto   **Seventh Position - Key of D Major**   Gebauer

The above Rondo appears in the Modern Guitar Method, Grade Two, Mel Bay System, as a study in 2nd position. It is an excellent study in 7th position in which the first finger (L. H.) is used freely. Note the movement from the D note, 7th fret 3rd string to the C♯, half tone lower on the 6th fret, same string and back to D on 7th fret. The first three lines of this Rondo designated as section "A" will be played in the key of D major. The next section, "B" is in D minor. Observe the "B♭" in the 3rd complete measure of the D minor part. This note is played by extending the 4th finger out of position to the 11th fret. Then play the "A" with the 3rd finger and the G♯ with the 2nd finger, returning to 7th position by playing the "A" with the 4th finger.

Old English With A Beat
Review First, Second and Third Position
Duet with Chord Acc.

72

The B Minor (Harmonic) Scale in Fourth and Fifth Position

Scale No. 1

The Same Scale in Sixth and Seventh Position

Scale No. 2

B Minor Study

Jazz Man Buys A Farm
A Review of First and Third Position

An Original by Roger Filiberto

The Scale of C Minor (Harmonic)
Third and Sixth Position

The Same Scale in Fifth and Sixth Position

The Same Scale in Seventh and Eighth Position

C Minor Etude

Practice in all Three Scales shown above.

THE NINTH POSITION

Ninth Position Study No. 1

The above study is played on the first three strings.

One Octave Scale of E Major - Ninth Position

Ninth Position Study No. 2
One Octave Only

Allegretto

Ninth Position Study No. 3
One Octave Only - First Three Strings

Waltz

77

Ninth Position Study No. 4

Ninth Position Study No. 5

Ninth Position Study
Including the Fourth and Fifth Strings

The complete Scale of A Major in Ninth Position

The Irish Washer Women
More in Ninth Position

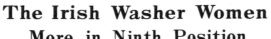

★ Observe the unusual fingering in this measure. Moving the first finger to D facilitates the reach to F♯ on the 14th fret. Note the use of the 2nd finger on the "E" 12th fret, sliding it back to "D" on 10th fret, returning you to 9th position.

Melody in Ninth Position

Observe ★ for unusual fingering.

★ The 3rd finger is not usually used on the "D" note (12th fret) in this position. Normally, the 4th finger is used for this note··· however, it would be necessary to move the 4th finger quickly over to the "B" note (12th fret 2nd string). This is awkward and not good form. hence the use of the 3rd finger in this particular situation. We recommend placing the 3rd and 4th fingers on the respective notes simultaneously as in a chord.

Bagatelle For Two (Goofin' off in C Major)

★ This sign means to repeat the TWO previous measures.

★★ You can have a little fun with this eight measure "release" through improvising a "take-off" of your own. Follow the instructions regarding the use of scales against the chords, observing the rules of starting and ending faithfully. Your teacher should be able to assist you at this point.

Chords in the 8 measure release are to be played as shown in the diagrams pictured at the bottom of this page.

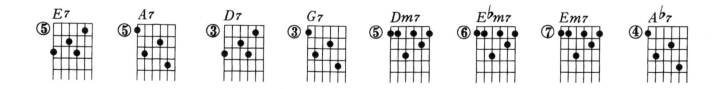

Ninth Position Study in E Major
On First Four Strings

Ninth Position Study in C♯ Minor

More in Ninth Position-E Major

★ The use of the 2nd finger here is optional⋯you can use the 1st finger, as well. This etude appears earlier in this book as a study in 4th position. The student can therefore choose which position is best for this study.

The Complete Scale of D major in Ninth Position

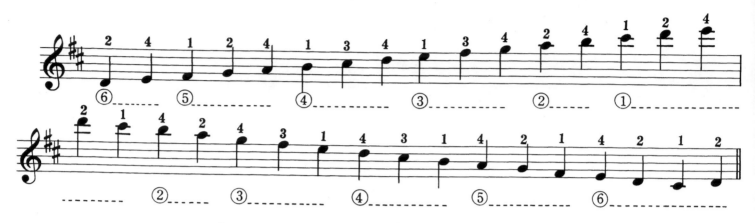

Scale Study in D Major··· Use same fingering as above.

Repeat five times.

Another Ninth Position Scale study in D Major

Practice the two above scale studies slowly at first, gradually picking up speed as you become more familiar with the position.

Mandolina - Ninth Position study in D major

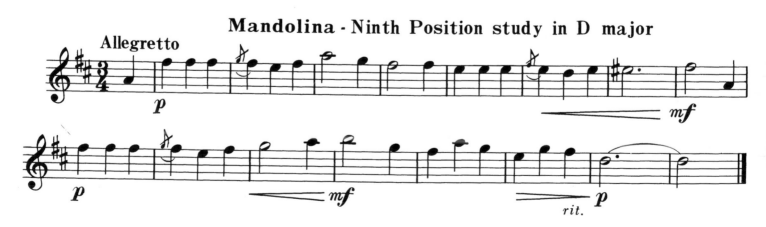

Sonatina
A Review of Fifth Position

Andante

Mazas
Arr. by Mel Bay

The Scale of D Minor(Harmonic)
Fifth and Eighth Position

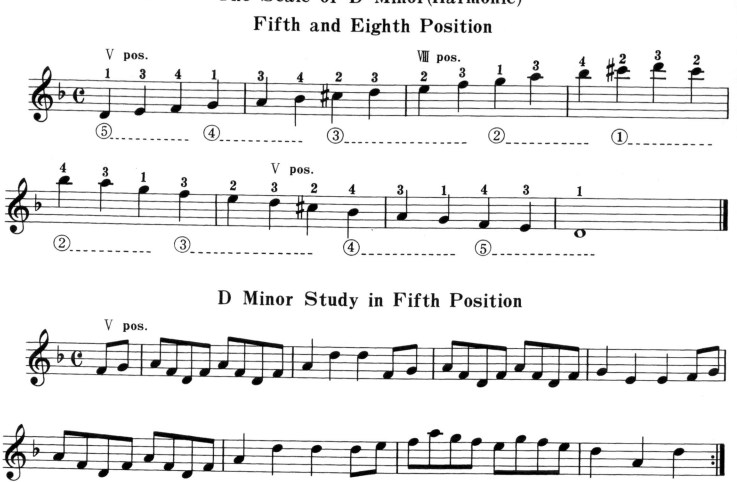

D Minor Study in Fifth Position

More in D Minor-Fifth Position

★ Hold 3rd finger down while playing the "a" note with the 2nd finger. This will make this passage a lot smoother.

Swingtime

Syncopation study in Fifth and First Position
with an occasional detour into Fourth Position.

An Original
by
Roger Filiberto

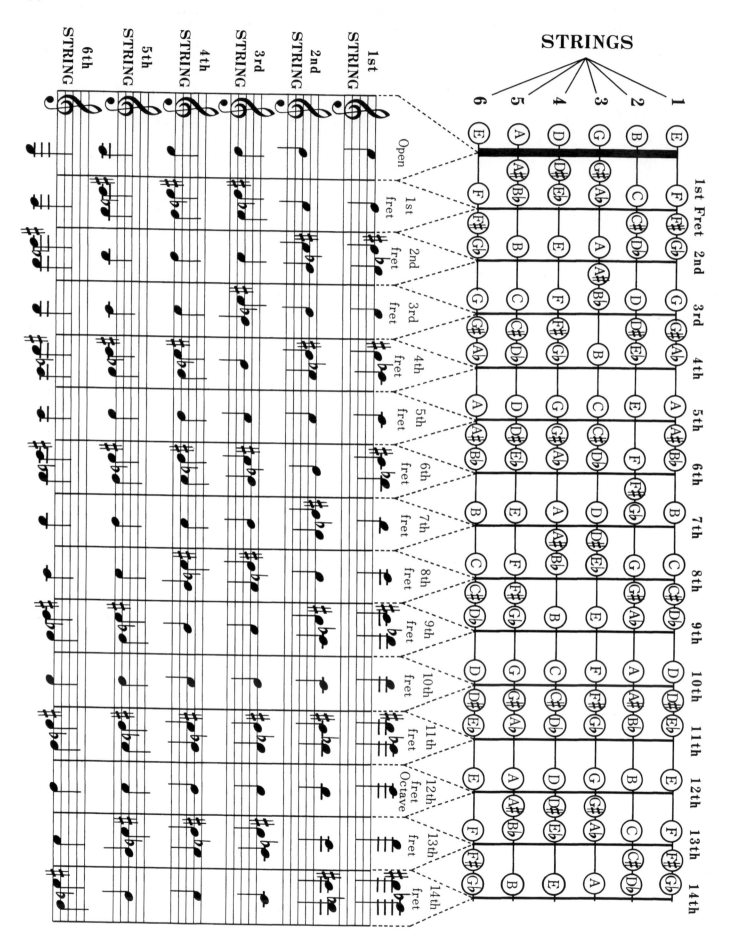

Guitar Fingerboard Chart